The Magic of Everything

IHSAN JONES

ISBN:0998513119
ISBN-13:9780998513119

DEDICATION

This book is dedicated to my family and friends, one of whom said, "I thought I knew you. I now, know you more and honor and respect your knowledge."
Thank you SG for your comments. You too have been an inspiration..

CONTENTS

ACKNOWLEDGMENTS

I am thankful to the universe for sending the signals. And to God for allowing them to sink in.
Grateful for the ones that lend support with love and admiration- All my children, family, and friends.

PREFACE

In this book, I give you tools to develop an acute
sense of awareness that can take you to greater
heights for unleashing the Magic that essentially has
inherently always belonged to you. The Magic of
Everything is about synergies that can resist
changing moments until it is peaked to perfection.
Encapsulated within the body, is the 'magic" that's
collaborated between the layers of the heart, mind,
and soul, with a chance for obstacles and
uncertainty. The tools that we explore can unleash

1

the hidden power to enable these forces to be released. By reconstructing Magic and how it happens, we can reclaim our ability to recapture the forces that are encapsulated in our inner cycles. Look deep within if you want to have the ability of increased performance that's peaked to perfection, and to enhance your insight by turning it into foresight. Who wouldn't love to turn magic around with the ability to have it work for us at the drop of a dime or at a moment's notice. I see magic as the hidden potential waiting to be harnessed to match its destiny. We do have the ability to control magic. We just have to learn how. This book uncovers the tools that are necessary to reveal the information that explains why the magic that's been there all along hasn't had its day in court. You also will develop an acute sense of awareness that would be needed to understand this message. Enjoy the

magic!

INTRO

There is magic in everything.

Everything we touch begins and ends with magic.

Magic is in our very fiber, our being. It is our soul

living through us -and playing tag. Our conscious

mind wants to control the magic. But it must first,

be caught. There are ways of capturing the magical

moments as we harness and release them. This book

is about the magic that happens and our willingness

to let it escape.

"Magic is the heart and soul creating laughter" IJ

"Synergies won't last, they fluctuate with time, but people do."

*People champion the noble causes that can alter the course.

"You might outlast the sentiments that you have today when you shift your perspectives for tomorrow."

*Sentiments are adjusted as we shift focus -but sometimes we might have just had a change of heart.

3 SHIFTING PERSPECTIVE

We could change a lot of things if we knew how. I'm not talking about changing things like clothes or shoes. What I am talking about is changing our minds. Changing our minds commands a lot of thinking. Like getting in touch with our sentiments and feelings. We must have a feeling or inkling first, before we make a conscious effort to change or shift focus. Why is shifting focus necessary? TO SOOTHE OUR BRAINWAVES THAT'S WHY. We get reprieve from overthinking if we get rest. We have to constantly tell ourselves that we can change, that we can do better, that we can make adjustments that are necessary to move us in the right direction. What we can't do is worry about the about the shoulda, coulda, woulda's. These are the things that will likely give us the most turmoil. Let me tell you a true story about myself so that we can get acquainted.

There was a time in my life when I needed to depend on somebody. No, not physically. Because when I looked around there was always someone in close enough proximity in person or by phone that I could pick up and dial to have conversation. What I'm talking about is that need for clarification. We all seem to have it from time to time. That's when we can pick up the phone line or muster up the courage to speak to God. To become weak at the knees and humbly submit to prayer. Prayer is a ritual we can't skip over if we want to talk to God. I get speech impediment when I perform the ritual because I don't always know what I want to say. But one day I did. In my most audible voice as loud and clear as could be heard in my heart…and with my mind, I spoke to God. I asked God about all the wonderful things that were happening in my life and the world. I also asked about the ones that weren't so pleasant. It was a general question in no specific context or order. Basically, I wanted to know. I wanted to know EVERYTHING. I begged and asked God again, over and over (with my speech impediment or stumbling words) how it is that everything's possible. My inquiries were of giant proportions and was mostly inaudible rhetoric breaking into waves or tones. This so called speech impediment (I didn't really have one. That's what I call it when I don't always know what to say), had me sounding like I was speaking in tongues or tongue tied and twisted. I'd often forget what it was I was trying to say-but I figured God might somehow hear me and the general nature of the message. That's when I realized that there is no right or wrong with prayer it's just important that you do it. On this one particular night I became so wrapped up in what I was saying (those inaudible words again) that it seemed to not make sense, except for begging and pleading that a break though would occur- in my consciousness to give me the answers I was seeking. I didn't go into prayer with false expectations. I knew there could be no one on one with God unless I opened up. So I went to prayer with an open mind, an open heart, sincerity, and a willingness to be receptive to whatever would come. In all honesty I must admit that I had tried this before. Attempting to connect without major distractions. That's why I always chose a quiet room. It's where I could be isolated. I wasn't a stranger to prayer. I had no problem with praying anywhere at any time because realistically, it was just a matter of closing my eyes (or not) and trying to concentrate. But I also had to listen. Listening for the inaudible sounds that might come back. On this night they did. I wasn't in crisis mode when I began this. There wasn't a sense of urgency, but like I said, this was a general inquiry into solitude and prayer. But the strangeness was there. I had kind of, already felt something special about the night. Then something happened. Something different. It was hard to explain, but I felt as if I had spoken to God, and that sound, or the inquiries were beginning to reverberate. It no longer felt like a one-way channel.

I was starting to feel the receptors and the power as if something was calling as the sky was opening. The darkened night lights of the sky were enveloping me. Then there was a resonating sound beam like stardom flickering in the star dust. In a raised sky, and me beneath it, I felt small, embellished, but intuitive. The sparkles were reminiscent of shooting stars that began to cast white lights. It felt like I was a rock star arriving on stage. The beams light sharpened focus and I remained in view. This was my early evening investment that paid off. I was in the midst of a profound experience that would have a chain reaction that couldn't be stopped. The channeling of energy was so strong that I received a rush of adrenaline. I became engulfed in the charm and wisdom of the moment. I was delighted as if a child and became feverish in my quest. The light still flickering, had spun brighter in this powerful moment. I knew that I had reached some sort of apex because when I emerged from this aura of inconspicuous inquiry, the subdued lighting returned and my eyes were no longer shut. I arose as a person with a greater understanding and new awakening. God had lit the way and opened up the sky for me I now believe it was a way of showing me then, that I would be able to see clearly and with focus. Dim lights surrounded by white, I became more fervor-ish. Sure, I've had my prayers answered before, but nothing so powerful as on this night. It was early evening, but dark outside. I had been recluse in the house all day attending to children and doing chores. I don't really know what compelled me to make this night special-or say a special prayer that would instigate a chain reaction.

I was moved in the process of this prayer.

Something different. Something that hadn't

occurred before. This night as I got lost in the

words- my vision had changed and I could see the

night sky inside my head with my eyes shut. The

stars were at a distance but surrounded me. My eyes

were tightly shut the more intense the prayer. Then

a flash of light appeared. Almost like a shooting star

except that it stayed lit. It was bright. I couldn't see

anything present or any forces but I sure felt them.

It felt like I was surrounded by a force capturing me

into oblivion. Taking me to a state beyond anything

I have ever seen. I knew at that moment there was

myself and God. Clearly I could see a magnificence

like no other time. It was magic. Something had

appeared and could not only feel the pain of my

inquiry but had filled a void of the gaps in space. This presence was surely felt. My mind had snapped attentively to honor what was there. No shapes, no forms, but stars and light. And a solitude like I had never felt. I was complacent in the moment to see and feel everything that there was. I took it in. Soaked it up like a sponge being wrought with water. My soul was dripping wet as I felt I had been drenched in LOVE. There was something kind there. Something that nature let me know wasn't as foreign as it would seem. The shadowy darkness let me know that I couldn't ACTUALLY see it. But the light beamed on my face like a flashlight generating from its source. It was an intense moment of anticipation with a clarification and commitment to let me see (things) going forward. I say this in retrospect now, but I was being prepared then for what was to come. There is a hymn that's familiar and many have sung it. It goes…mine eyes have seen the glory of the coming of the Lord". For me…God was there. I take it to heart what it means to have a communion with God. It's something that's very personal.

As we get to the magic, which is the topic of this book, I can share with you, ways of how we can attempt to control and harness that force that God gives us as a gift. And although my speech impediment only lasts through prayer- I usually know what it is specifically I am seeking deep down inside. It is that God will help me release the magic every time. Magic can be- miracles, magic can be blessings. We can talk all day about what magic is or isn't. But most importantly, magic is the unseen force that allows us a break though in our most critical time of need. Magic is always good, when associated with the divine. In this book, I tell you how to "catch" the magic.

4 CAPTURING THE MAGIC

The magic never dies. Magic is the power we have within us that arrives in the nick of time in a do or die situation. We have to sink or swim as we call it. Some want to attribute magic to luck but I for one know that this is not possible. Luck is a wish. Magic is an action. Magic is that element that we can have control over once we know how. A few things to explain here are luck, inspiration, and magic. These are mutually exclusive terms and each has its own place and peak in a given situation. Take luck for example. Does luck run out? Can luck actually

leave or can we lose the midas touch? Luck is time

synched up with preparedness. Many people have

shown their infatuation with luck or being lucky of

some kind. There might be a strong correlation

between luck and what is called "good" timing. I do

believe that we all can be lucky and also can

experience a lucky streak. Luck will come and go.

Then there is inspiration. Having the right

inspiration can lead you to ramp up the speed

required for you to receive luck. A lucky individual

is also one who has likely been inspired. Inspiration

comes in many forms-flattery, chivalry, kind words

or acts and deeds. But mostly, inspiration is

something that stirred you in a way that makes you

believe or have faith. When you can have faith then

you can act on that courage and are more

susceptible to achievement. Inspiration is a prelude to courage and confidence, while luck is given freely as an incentive to make you believe. And magic is made up of both of them. We are inspired by magic and we need luck to synch up the time elements so that magic can do its thing. Can we touch magic? Can we see magic? No. But it's just like the time when I was in prayer and everything came before me that was beautiful and I had spoken to God. I was in the presence of something omnificent and the magic will happen the same way. God's presence had appeared suddenly out of nowhere and seemingly from nothing. The magic does happen. It is a bright light shining through the darkness along with stars while sparks are flying everywhere and generating a buzz. You might even hear a humming sound once the magic has hit your eardrums as your heart races to pace itself with the dance. Magic is a ritual. It is our soul stirring, giving us power to outlast even the forces on the scale and magnitude of an earthquake. Magic is an illusion that we make when we need it the most. Sleeping dormant- acting as a quiet spot that shouldn't be disturbed until it's time to let us know how powerful it, and we are, in the eyes of God. It is our gift.

Can you imagine leveraging your greatest power? Can you imagine capturing something that you can't touch or feel or see- except maybe to hold onto it long enough to put it to use? The magic is always there. We have to let it perform. Why does the magic seem separate from our person? It's not. It's that the soul has always been the force to reach out in our time of need. If we left it to our thought processes or conscious-we'd tap out. We would not be in tune with those forces that give us the ability to react with the unseen because first, we would talk ourselves out of it. Why should we delve into the minds inner most forces that we somehow think can trick us? We might think our mind is playing tricks on us therefore we will not try to capture or harness that which is real. We are given signs all along that the soul is onto something and our minds haven't understood what the messages are yet for lack of clarity. It's because we don't tend to speak in riddles. We don't necessarily react until those warning signals become intense enough to force us to pay attention. They are like the speech impediment I experienced when praying. I got lost in the high altitude of the ritual so much so that I had to actually lose myself again through conscious awareness in order to have a break through. Unless the signs are really clear, we most likely won't pay attention. It will be like the little birdie in your head saying. "I told you so". We could have been warned over and over about something many times-but many of us aren't sharp enough to lend focus until after the fact. We won't pay attention. It is in retrospect that we learn most of our lessons. Even if the voices (in our head) have already chimed in.

2017

2017. It's the presidential election and the race was becoming intense. I was getting caught up in the cross fire and it almost didn't matter which side you were routing for because the atmosphere was shaky both ways. I had a vested interest this time around because I wanted to see our first woman president in the white house. It became obvious that this wasn't going to happen as it got down to the wire. Right before I heard the results a dark cloud came over me. So much so that I had shared it with my daughter who was also becoming disappointed with the results. I went to bed early hoping that I wasn't waking up to a nightmare. I told her that I had a dream that night (the night of the election) that something was amiss. Something was off and I felt it. I told her that I couldn't put my finger on it but I knew that something large scale was going to happen that's affecting the mood. Outside there was a noticeable change in the weather. It had shifted to become cloudy and dark just like the mood that was simmering. Usually when I have intensified dreams like this they have a tendency to bare out. I was hoping for the good of everything I could muster that this feeling would shake and the mood would pass. It felt depressing and I was scared that something would happen. I had told her it was something big. Something earth shaking and of a large scale magnitude. But I still…didn't know what it could be. Time seemed to lapse as I sat alone at the table in solitude wondering how come the forces that were working inside of me no one else could feel. When I finally decided that I could live with what happened (in the election) I turned on my phone whom I had sworn I wouldn't pick up. No social media, no TV, no nothing. Just quiet and solitude until I could figure this out. Half the morning had passed before I decided to look up the news on my cell phone. "Massive protests in major cities all around the country. People forming into crowds and piling into the streets. The mood had changed and the sudden shock of the first woman not being able to hold the position in the white house as the 45th President of the United States had sunk in. People weren't taking it well. I could feel their pain. All along, this is what it was leading to. Those thoughts and premonitions. The mood swing and the dream. I had been given pre-warning of the event. I had known a long time ago since I was a little girl that I was intuitive and could see things before they took place. But the ability I didn't have was to PREVENT anything from happening that I might have suspected or known about. This is what has prompted me to write this book and explain what I feel is called the magic principle that occurs before and leading up to an event. We can capture it. Why? It is an element that exists and we are always given warning signs that lead up to it. This book will focus on the majestic aspect because that is the inspiration and lucky feeling that God has given us whenever we do experience the magic. This particular story is about the feelings of disappointment with the election and that there were warning signs all along that I could have noticed. We have them all the time. Warning signs. But what we don't likely have is a keen sense of awareness with the ability to act on them. To alter the course, so to speak, so that they can take another direction. If we could somehow intervene with fate? I think we would.

I could clearly see that my dreams had led to showing me that massive display of disappointment. I dismissed it and thought no more of it even though there were more days of unrest. I still had that angst in my gut although the election had passed. What I did do however, was watch the news and keep pace with what everybody was saying (news, media, etc.). Then something started happening-again. I began to see little images of what I call cartoons. They would just crop in my head from time to time, no big deal. I certainly wasn't focusing on them just noticing that I kept seeing this one particular image more regularly, at least once a day. I'm sure I had already formed my opinion about things in the wake of my own disappointment but the image I couldn't shake. That image was of pinnochio growing his nose. It kept growing longer and longer each time I'd see it. Hum, I thought in a fleeting moment. Why do I keep seeing that? I actually said it once - to one of my youngest grandchildren-telling them about the image. Why do I keep seeing pinnichio in my head? They were amused it appeared but I'm sure paid no real attention to what I had said. I wasn't focusing on it either except that I was starting to recognize that I was capturing the image. For those people that believe that thoughts are fleeting and meaningless, this might be proof that if we hone in on what's actually drawing our attention, then it might be something worth paying attention to. I'm like your average person. Of course I imagined it as a fleeting thought but still recognized that it stood out as strange. Then it happened. My littlest granddaughters in the house- the twins, decided they wanted me to read them a book. This was NOT the same set of granddaughters that I had talked about or mentioned before. These were the littlest babies and they were only three years old. One of them ran up to me happy go lucky as if she had found her favorite

storyteller-grandma! "Grandma, can you read this?'

"Yes, honey", I gladly responded, as I usually

would when they'd ask me.

 I finally was able to put a context to pinnochio. It

seemed that many accusations were being hailed

back and forth in the news and it was becoming

much harder to discern what was being told that

was truthful and what was not. Pinnichio was a

reference to the climate and the atmosphere

surrounding the election and I had gotten my

answer. If I had only followed the cues I would

have known in advance that this election was going

to be hard to follow. That is the purpose sometimes

of us receiving warning signals about something

that we might feel passionate or intense about. In

the end it didn't really matter who won, it was about

what was being said. Do I know if there were any lies being told? There is no way I could tell. Only pinnochio would know that.

There are two terms I'd like to introduce you to. One is Intra Gleaning and the other is Ultra-Gleaning. These two concepts are both ways to tap into the spirit and gather that essence of consciousness that seeks to harness the unbridled spirit or soul. You can further develop these inclinations and explore them from heightened awareness. Maybe they can act as an intervention. Maybe, just maybe, they are helpful in other aspects of life a well. Intra- gleaning and ultra-gleaning are terms that I am describing as useful for how we will be looking at "capturing magic".

To capture the magic- two things must happen. We should get ourselves in a state of readiness or make preparation as we do when we pray. Then we need to focus so intensely and concentrate to achieve this thing while ridding ourselves of mistrustful thinking. It will take a distraction in order to regain our focus and release the positive awareness or attraction of magic. What do you mean by distraction? I thought that magic just happens. Well, the magic does just happen, but it is us getting rid of our annoyances that unleash what magically happens in the soul.

5 SOUL CLEANSING

In faith, there is what's known as soul cleansing.
Soul cleansing is a way of ridding devices and self-
destructive habits. Souls cleansing is powerful and
it's a way to connect with God. If you soul cleanse
then you are intensely praying and asking God's
forgiveness for everything. Only you can identify
what you seek, and only you can rectify that with
God. Most of us seek peace and harmony as well as
love for all mankind and brethren. If you are not
praying for that then you are not likely trying to

cleanse the entire soul. Soul cleansing involves two steps. One is with prayer. The other is through meditation. There may be other ways to soul cleanse. These are the ways that I am familiar with. This book is not to steer or define YOUR purpose. It is only to share the knowledge that can get you to the magic. We all have our faith principles that guide us. They should be based on your beliefs. Sharing our faith principles can only strengthen us, they don't dilute or take away from them in any aspect. In the end it is your choice of how you make that connection. Soul cleansing supersedes the rituals and helps with defining purpose. Soul Cleaning can help not only to discover the magic, but to intra- glean and ultra-glean as well. Learning about them can help you in many ways.

I came to know about intra gleaning through trial

and error. It is much like the other warning signs I get about small things. Those small things turn into big things once understood. So intra-gleaning is a concept that I developed.

Intra-Gleaning is a way of having a steady response to outer stimulus.

Ultra-Gleaning is to sharply focus and to gain shifts in perspective.

It is a cause and effect state like what occurs when everything happens succinctly. It is knowing that you are ready like the example of when God manifest when I was deeply in prayer. When you are enveloped in thought and the intensity is increasing-you will have to eventually let go to release the pressure. This is where I think ultra-gleaning is affective. It releases the pressure at the right moment so that the magic can take over. The magic knows the precise time to appear and is released through your soul. You feel the weight and passion at the height of awareness but only once the pressure has been released. Hey, wait a minute. Isn't that contradictory to what you just said about the magic happening naturally? And shouldn't that be the opposite based on all that's been said and what we know, that concentration should not be broken when you are trying to achieve something, in fact, it should be ramped up harder? Based on my experiences and which is the purpose of this book, I am telling you that is NOT the case. Too often we have thought that practice without distraction is what brings success. While I had previously thought this way before I now have evidence to the contrary. Let me share with you my game scenario.

I have a habit of playing games. Mostly, I play the

games on my cell phone because it is small compact and convenient. Since I will have the phone in my hand I can take the game anywhere I want to go. I might be playing in the car, while sitting by the pool at the YMCA, or even to the beach. The point is, I play games for fun but I also get wrapped up in my games real intensely. I'm sure there are many folks that find solitude or get some kind of relief or relaxation from playing games. It is not a job, so it is downtime for me. Most likely, I do it to have fun. Here is what I discovered- but, this discovery didn't happen overnight. Just as I have had many signals, messages, or warning signs about many things, these games turned out to be no exception. It reminds me of the book I read, Pinnochio, when I was reading it to my granddaughters-'Why can't a book be a book? Why did it have to relate to something so astronomically heavy like an election race? My same way of thinking about the games was, "Well, why can't a game just be a game? Why do I have to put more into it? There is a GOOD reason. It's called Head-weights. Head-weights are the exercises we do to help with our intra and ultra-gleaning. I'll explain more about head-weights later. For now, let's continue on regarding the games. So it was my favorite pastime that turned into my biggest conniption (aside from that one time in prayer when I became closer to God). I was playing on this particular occasion a bubble game it's a shoot the bubble towards the right color type of game in order to make a match and clear the field. Each level gets harder and harder with more obstacles. The funny thing is that I was noticing a pattern. I was receiving little signals or warning signals about how I was playing the game. Now mind you, I have played these types of games for years before now having the ability to pinpoint my skill. I was so used to playing that once I had cleared a level I would be on auto-pilot trying to clear the next one. While intensely focused on the game my sub-conscious would get lost on certain moves. Those moves that I was most distracted on were the ones that could enable me to win. The winning shot is what it's called. I began to notice that every time I got closer to the kill shot my level of concentration would deter while on my greatest moment. I was about to be triumphant and win if only I could stay focused! But it was through this transposition or junction, that I would usually (unbeknownst to me) have a shift in consciousness and could be distracted just enough to execute! The execution would be perfect too because it enabled me to win however I wasn't privy to the "dunk shot" as I call it.

OK. Sure. In all fairness, I have to say that there are several times when I can recall intensely focusing on winning enough to get good enough at it to make myself learn the so called trick shots that would be needed to win. Although they varied from game to game and level to level. It took practice. Intense practice. And a whole lot of skill. So I was actually able to see the final shot on many occasions and was just as elated when I won when I didn't see the winning shot. But the point of the story is to show you how magic relates to being released at the right moment. The pattern I was shown was that I was able to develop a knack for winning even when my moment of concentration was lost. This may have been through practice or dreaming about winning and wanting it so bad. They say that you must have a vision of winning first in order to do it. I do believe that. But I also believe that through my faith, wisdom, and loads of practice, I've been able to develop a skill that hones the point of releasing what is called "magic". The magic principles have worked for me- they are having an acute awareness of the precise time of execution but having to release or give up "control" of that execution and let another force take over. That force is the soul that is releasing the magic as its always wanted to do. Your soul is like a valiant soldier rising to the occasion of stepping in when you can allow it to. It is magic pure and simple.

The soul is illusive. The soul has always been illusive and we have tried to catch it. The soul works day and night but the soul wants to remain free so that it is unencumbered with the day to day rituals of outer influence. The soul is our comfort. It is also our savior. The soul is the magic and the gift that God has given to us to use at will. The soul, thus far has not been captured, the soul remains aloof so that when everything else fades, it can remain, ready, willing, and able, to play. My soul took over for me and executed the shot but I wasn't able to release it until I had given up (through temporary distraction) the concentration or control. How can the soul be the trickster and the hero at the same time? The soul is not the trickster or the hero, the soul is the magic. There are two purposes to this book. One is to teach you about the magic and the signs or warning signals that we get about things in advance. The other is to give you the tools and how

41

you can apply them in order to harness what we are naturally gifted with.

If a basketball player throws the ball in the last few seconds of the game and he or she is half court, what do you think it's going to take for them to make the shot? Don't worry, I'll say it for you. It's going to take a miracle. Maybe the player is as good as they come, might be top of their game. Practice upon practice makes perfect, right? Yes, and no. Yes, It's true that if you keep practicing something over and over again you will eventually get good at it and maybe even become an expert. But there is also the element of surprise; the minute when the magic happens. We don't know that just because the player is an expert that he will make a free throw shot from half court away from the net with surmounting opposition. We can only hope that he

gets a break and shoots his best shot for the win.
These are often the intensified moments we live for
when playing a game. The adrenaline rush, passions
are running high, people are watching and intensely
focused on the game. Well guess what? Anything
can happen. But if the ball does hit the net and fall
through, then everyone (except the opposite team)
will be ecstatic. He or she will be dubbed as king or
queen, but definitely not rookie. Luck happens.
Inspiration happens. But when it's combined-its
magic. The basketball player was likely inspired to
work out previously before the game so that he
could learn to execute a long shot. He became lucky
that he was handed the ball and not someone else so
that if he made it he could become the hero. Now,
this player may or may not have become distracted
at the precise moment of releasing the ball. This is

something we can only entertain guessing unless we interview them. Like I mentioned before, there have been times when I was able to concentrate and actually "see" myself taking the last shot. But I'd venture to say that this player most likely didn't and although may have seemed focus was distracted long enough to give it up to faith when he threw it. There is no way he could see inside of the net, but he had to know approximately where it was. He had practiced before and was in the general vicinity of making it. His hands knew the action, how much pressure to apply and then some. But magic wouldn't be magic if it told you its secret. The secret is that magic comes from the soul. The player's soul took over and where he may or may not have procrastinated or hesitated, the soul knew that he needed to finish and decided to come out from its space and place the ball right into the basket. I bet the player was just as surprised as the audience was. He may or may not have seen or recall the precise moment of execution.

There are two types of distraction. One is the type where your mind has totally left whatever it is you were doing and so you miss the mark or have an accident. Maybe you caught yourself in time-who knows. This type of distraction doesn't (intentionally) release the soul. Remember the soul is not a savior, but it a saving grace. The soul is the actual magic. The soul sees what the consciousness can't so they collude from time to time but in opposite spheres. The soul has great timing to release the magic. But the magic must appear as a mirage in order to remain elusive, otherwise you wouldn't be able to see its miraculous affects.

Timing makes perfect, and when it comes to magic, there is no better way to display it.

Where's my proof? In my games. Many times I won without seeing exactly how I had done it. My hands were moving. I knew all the moves and the shots to take to burst the bubbles. I even had good concentration with nothing that I thought could distract me. This kind of distraction is unwanted distraction and will probably make you lose the game. But there's another kind of distraction that's temporary, very brief, it actually should be called deterrence. It is when the mind veers into something oblivious in order for the soul to break through. The soul is there for you routing for you in the game but it also cannot work while you are having head play (or thoughts that's can't release it. So it pulls your brainwaves over to something else, just a little, and long enough so that it can do its part. The soul loves to execute. It's just that we think too much about the execution part that we can sometimes miss the mark. To release the soul, you would need to free up some space in order to release the magic. That way you can make the shot even if you can't put your finger on exactly how it was done.

 So how do we know that its magic and how can we harness it? Why should we even bother, or care? These are two important questions. And why I should share another story.

I want to share the story that leads me to explain why magic is purposeful and why it could be released through ultra-gleaning, once it is recognized, in order to be captured.

6 THE MIRAGE

A mirage is something we think we see but often times don't. A mirage can be something that's placed in your way on purpose. The very idea of seeing or witnessing a mirage is as a substitute for something else. Maybe our senses are so acute that the thing does exist beyond our mind. It is not likely, but we would most likely find out the hard way. Through the senses we feel, and sight is a part of that.

Sometimes we dig ourselves into little holes when we are thinking about something too much. That's when we can clear our minds by focusing on ultra-Gleaning which is the best way to override any shortcomings.

"If only I had known" is something we commonly say. Not just for mistakes but when we have seen an opportunity pass us by. All of this when we can have ultra-gleaning at our disposal.

Magic is a buzz word for illusive. We can never capture magic it seems because it alludes us. Magic is that thing. You know, that thing that everybody wants to talk about -let alone have. That magical mysterious drumroll that beats at the right time or better yet puts us in the right place at the right moment. It is a dream that manifests with rhythmic dances.

Our way of regaining our thoughts is to shift focus as if we're blaming ourselves as to how we responded to outside stimuli when in fact these are only thoughts in our heads. We can't blame ourselves for everything. Especially when it is out of our control. When our thought processes don't match- that doesn't mean we have to regain control about everything. We are not out of sync- we are doing what is called ultra-gleaning, to regain perspective.

To do ultra-gleaning, we must first do intra-cleaning. As these terms are new to you. I will explain them so that you will become familiar. Regaining retrospect is a sharper way of looking at things. We can call this ultra-gleaning because no matter what we thought-we either didn't or couldn't change the outcome.

"We don't need to focus on everything that crosses our mind. Only those that can shift or change our perspective. We can't collude with every force that's unseen, but we can become willing participants."

To ultra-glean a thought process, you must first inner- cleanse for awareness. A sharper focus can gain perspective but filtering shifts alignment. Let's face it. There are many thoughts going through our head. We cannot concentrate on all of these thoughts at once. But there are some thoughts that are specifically trying to give notice about things that are happening outside. A thought is just a thought you say. A thought is more than that. It is reaction to the synergies that have been catapulted in action. These actions may be happening now or in the future. When your future is at stake you likely want to do something about it. But to live once is to have lived twice, or not at all. Why do I say this? Because it shifts focus. It ultra-gleans on the thought process that matters and not the ones that don't. It shifts the alignment of having known to the forefront where it can bear fruit. The thought that comes to fruition is afterthought. It is when you think, "I wish".

How is ultra-gleaning so different from prayer or meditation?

Prayer is transcendental. Meditation is conformity and helps us with honing the circuits. Both take up areas in the spiritual realm in the mind that's calling from past and present. Both are about bringing insight or awareness into the future. How we choose to connect, is an individual and personal experience. Ultra-gleaning is a combination of them both and then some. Ultra-gleaning is rectifying a "lost" part of what's happening within the soul while it's trying to catch up.

Shifts in the brain don't happen because we tell them to. Shifts in the brain happen because they were always capable of reconnecting. Life's patterns are being dictated all the time. But we can't understand them all at once. It is through dictation that our inner world can see things that happen before and after. The "Lost" parts of our life, are patterns trying to shift. These waves are constant signals in our brain telling us that something wants to be let go or released via intuition and other processes like memory. We have the ability to recall "lost" parts and put them in perspective. When we do that, it can shift our focus. We can become more sharply aligned, intuitively, with what is being conveyed.

To ultra-glean, we need help. First it is with prayer. Then it is with developing an understanding that we are not in this alone and therefore cannot do this by ourselves. We are essentially acknowledging not only the existence of a higher being(force) but also developing a pattern of sharper focus. In the process we may or may not hone in on what's really driving us. It's like the scenery when you're taking a long trip. You will miss some of the scenery because it's not all meant to be taken in. A general perspective is sometimes good enough. Even a general reference as to the landscape or your surroundings. But ultra-gleaning gives you the posture that understanding where the peaks and valleys rise and fall will help navigate the terrain.

That is what ultra-gleaning is all about; helping us

to navigate the landscape within by giving sharper

focus, and better alignment to become in tune with

our bodies signals and intuition.

Personalities have nothing to do with ultra and intra

perspectives. They are not dependent internally on

our outside navigation because the inner forces are

subsets of the terrain in which we live. The outside

forces are dependent upon the intra and ultra to

eventually be freed up. When this happens, a whole

new world is at our disposal because it will reflect a

brighter or enlightened understanding of the way

things are or can and will be. If we can understand

what is happening inside when we feel the forces of

nature trying to pull us towards it-then we will grow

as individuals from the space in which we once

were. Evolution, to us, should be like shedding the skin and becoming a new person.

With intra gleaning, you are capturing the image. With ultra-gleaning you are capturing the mirage. The mirage is the mirrored part of what the soul is trying to do. It is the "lost soul" or connection that runs free. It is not trying to escape but it can be elusive until you catch whatever it is its trying to warn or tell you. It can at times still catch up. This is usually in retrospect, after it has appeared a dozen times sending its messages. The soul can become weary or otherwise known as lost. If you can catch the messages before time runs out (on the clock) the souls mission, or magic is complete. The message is only relevant for a stated time because it's related to a particular situation. If the situation no longer becomes relevant, then the message remains at bay as a lost cause. That is essentially the lost part. It is not that we as people are lost and our souls are running free. It's the opposite, which is, by understanding our purposes, we can catch up with it. Wouldn't it be great if we didn't have to play "cat and mouse". The great mind has to escape or become clouded in order for the soul to have the room and space it needs to perform. When I say that I'm just the messenger, I truly mean that. Remember, it is by trial and error that I was able to connect the dots. Mostly faith driven, the pieces of the puzzle fell together. I think God wanted me to know the importance of the connection so that I can pass it on to you. Now let me explain the tools that I think can help you with that connection.

7 HEADWEIGHTS

If you can remember that the premise of this book is

to exercise. Exercise through the faith principles

that you were taught and apply the techniques

which are called intra, and ultra- gleaning to help

you become more focused. I mentioned earlier

about head-weights. Head weights are the brains

patterns that clear up the fogginess. We all have our

fuzzy days and intra and ultra can help you. So can

exercising your head weights. We need to use head

weights to strengthen the brain muscles to ensure

they can respond at the proper time-timing is

EVERYTHING. It must be applied with accuracy

and precision so that even if you're not aware-your

head weights have strengthened the muscle so

sharply that it can capture what the soul is doing at

a moment's notice.

Imagine a speeding car high up in the mountains

having to make a turn. The corner is sharp and the

driver has no idea what to expect. Because timing is

everything the man will have to depend upon his

experience and training to get himself through the

situation. The driver can't see what's happening up

ahead. Will the road have debris in it? Is he facing

an obstacle? These are the elements of magic when

there is unexpected change. The driver will just

have to take his chances and slow down the car or

try to make the turn based on all he knows about

turning a corner while driving. GOOD LUCK!

Now, we see that word luck again. We know that

luck is only HALF of the equation. To have magic,

or perform a miracle-he will need to make the

curve. A prayer. A wish. All part of what he might

be doing as he's staring up the road. An experienced

driver might take a calculated chance that he could

make it. Doesn't mean that he will- just means the

odds are more stacked in his favor. A rookie who

might want to prove to himself that he can get

better, might take that chance anyway knowing that

it is a 50/50 risk. The point is that skills do matter.

So does training. I think it's foolish to take a risk

like that since the consequences could be going over

the side of the cliff! But who am I to say that it

should or shouldn't be done. Risk is risk, no matter

what the odds are. But you must admit that a

calculated risk at least leans the odds more in your favor. So training with head weights can help you prepare to develop precision with accuracy when you are attempting to do something. Either way, our confidence level is not particularly an indicator of our skills. Only by what we have demonstrated in the past, can we gauge ourselves going forward. No one would dare the driver to do this. If they did they would be just as foolish as he was. But the corner will be there, it's not likely that the road will change it will appear steady unless there's debris, or some sort of obstacle. When I talk about the magic I am not talking about taking chances. I'm talking about preparation for taking chances or being able to perform under duress or any other circumstances. The more practice you get with head weights, the more skilled you become when you are faced with a do or die situation. The magic and the soul are intertwined. Your soul would be affected deeply once you have performed the magic! So apply head weights whenever you get the chance. Head weight exercises are done to increase the chances or possibilities of understanding what the soul is already telling you- "this is going to happen, or that". Its giving you warning signals passing them off as signs that you are familiar with. Now all you have to do is take heed and harness them at the right moment to blend with what you already know in your soul. The soul is the assistant ready to make the swap. The soul is doing what it's supposed to do, which is waiting for the opportune time to save us. It takes a calculated- estimated risk based on your skills and training level. Freedom comes at a price. We have to pay a price to not have inhibition. When you speak to the soul you are giving up control. Yes, the soul is a part of you, but it's the part that has free reign. A lot of times we are scared to let the soul "Jump in". We will inhibit the thought as soon as it comes to the forefront. What if? We want to imagine the scenarios but we don't necessarily want to take a calculated risk. We want a sure shot! We want precision and accuracy. We want freedom to pull out the magic at a moment's notice and make it work for us every time. We can get close to it, but I'm telling you right now, it's not going to work. The magic will remain as 50/50 until we can incrementally increase the odds. We do this by our heavy lifting of head weights. Remember, prayer hones the skill (by increasing our faith). Meditation, helps (by increasing concentration) with good decision making. Soul cleansing should have already occurred because you would have needed to approach them both -with good intentions. Having control is another aspect of intra-gleaning and ultra-gleaning. And since they are all in collusion, it can decrease the anxiety or the fear of the magic not ever working

A true story-

I was driving down the freeway one day and I heard a loud horn. My mind had escaped from what I was doing momentarily, which of course, was driving. Who would want to release their thoughts at a time when they needed them the most? If ever I needed to be keeping my eyes on the road and thinking about driving, the time would be now. But somehow, my mind had freed up space and was concentrating on something else. This is not the "first kind of distraction" that I was explaining where something has diverted your attention. An attention grabber to throw you off balance to have you make a mistake. This is that "second form of distraction" or an aversion. This type does it completely on its own and is because the soul is beckoning to save you. There is something that's there that you are supposed to know about. It's up to you- after it's reached its apex- if you can figure it out. The aversion (not diversion) was a tactic of the lost soul. You had essentially switched gears to let it escape. The soul always gives forewarnings that is also its purpose. When you say, "I've touched someone's soul", what you are saying is that you probably got through to them and reached them where it counts. A deeper connection will have been deposited into the bank account of time in order for you to use it again and again. It will be up to you to have the courage to pull from those vaults during your trials and tribulations when you're tested. The vault represents a journey of how often and how much you can fill it. It will continue throughout your life cycle until the soul has reached its apex or your body has been worn out. They say wisdom comes with age. Well so does the spirit that carries the angel inside of us that touches the soul to release the magic. The soul represents awakening, awareness, and it is a beautiful consultant that knows how we feel, about EVERYTHING. That is why everything can be awakened or stirred inside via our senses. The soul is the embodiment of the feelings magnified that allow us to make choices that we can learn from. Now, as often as we can apply our head weights is how often we can capture the spirit (soul). It is a ginormous task, and takes a commitment. Using our head- weights affects the body's total outer stimuli because it increases reaction time ten-fold.

Here's a head-weight example: you have been projecting an image. You know that the image is clear to you because you have seen it before. The problem is that you might not have a frame of reference or context in which the image should be placed. First, we have to recognize displacement. Second, we have to know that the image is a mirage because it cannot be the actual physical thing. Third, we must think about the things that the symbol, image, item can represent. Then we write this down.

It should start off as an exercise:

I saw an image of a _____. It showed up around _____-(e.g. 2pm)

It kept showing up on these particular days. The image has NOT gone away yet.

This is the first part of the process of applying head-weights.

I must caution you at this point that if God wants you to know something, you will get the message one way or another. We are not trying to intercept God's communications, but we have to know that it is God trying to stir the soul. The soul is warning us so that we can figure it out. Don't ask me why we do not have direct communication (from God). That is not for me to answer. I can only share with you my experiences and tell you what I know. If we take heed and practice the process of writing and jotting it down, each time something would happen, we have a better chance of honing the skills in order to "capture" that understanding, if nothing else. We may also develop the ability to intervene. Who knows? Only time will tell with the proper training and gleaning the results.

(True story) cont…

In the car, when the horn blew, it brought me back to my senses. I wasn't headed for an accident however, quite the opposite. It appeared that I had been safe the entire time. In my most vulnerable state, for some reason due to the soul awakening me, I was safe. This was a conscious moment. And the perfect driving record that I had for years was contributing to me staying on pace and not drifting into other lanes, nor hitting other cars. There is actually more to that story (a true story) and I wrote about it in another book called, "When Crows Call". But for the explanations and purpose needed here, I have shortened this part of the story to serve its purpose. I didn't get hurt that day. I didn't get into a crash. I don't even think I had a close call until I heard the horn and upon waking from the fog. However, I was averted. Averted while I was actually driving. This was a miracle. A true diversion would have probably killed me. But a temporary restraint placed on my (thinking) mind caused it to roam but not carelessly, only so that whatever message was trying to get through-I would get. The magic was also at bay waiting to perform if I had needed it. Luckily, I didn't. I will be using my head weights to sort out the episode. Writing it down to weigh in on this incidental occurrence. I would like to concentrate more on what I was thinking at the time I was averted. Maybe it correlates to other events. In my other book I explained exactly what those thoughts related to. But for purposes here, it is to show you "how" to use the head weights.

8 EXCHANGE(OF THOUGHTS)

This back and forth exchange is what we want to work on. Following Gods cues. It's the dialogue of back and forth exchange that will prompt us to write our stories, clues, or incidents down. The clues are leading to a presentation so we must sort them out. It would have been easier to follow the pinnochio clues if I had been writing them down. The images kept popping up but I thought there was no context, or frame of reference. Little did I know that Everything was staring me right in the face. On the news, on the internet. I could have put two and two together long ago that they were related to the election. Maybe I wouldn't have been so surprised. The advantage however, was that it was given as foresight. I was allowed to "feel" the mood of a mass number of people which made me in synch with my intuition. The soul knew that I was passionate about something. The soul was preparing me for what I would consider, something that would be worse. I would likely have caught on long before if I had written them down.

The MAGIC has perfect execution. Perfect timing as they say. That, and the soul's intervention into our recurring affairs, like pinnochio, and so many others. My stealthy driving habits while driving down the street, the games I play, ever so often, and that which wakes me, like the loud noise (horn) to

prevent any possible accidents. Aversion is real.
Aversion is the part we can't avoid but it is what is
needed to release the Magic. We can understand it
better (how it's used) if we can just get used to
reading the signs or cues- in other parts of our lives.
Also capturing the magic when it happens by
writing it down. Did the magic happen after an
aversion or before? Can I actually recall what it was
that helped me to execute (with precision) in that
magic moment? If I can write down the images,
then they might no longer be a mirage and serve as
a base for writing the clues. OK. In actuality, we
probably cannot ever capture the magic. But we can
increase the chance of it HAPPENING more often.
After all-if the magic could be caught- it probably
would no longer be considered "MAGIC". In the
mean-time…lets increase our head weights in order

to increase our power of intuition and to ultra- glean

our spirit so that we can be in tune with our bodies

and make a deeper connection.

On the following pages are exercises that can help

you. Try them!

Take heed and try to identify and recognize the

patterns that can help you get to the magic. The

process is one and the same to hone the skills to

increase the magic AND to better recognize the

patterns or clues that are leading up to an event.

You should be able to know about the event ahead

of time (which increases your power of intuition)

and you can also use ultra- gleaning to hone the

senses. Your intra-gleaning may already have been

working through prayer and whatever daily rituals

you use for inspiration. If you can know the

patterns, then overtime you can develop the senses

to sharpen the mechanism that can fine tune the soul. They come from the same source. The messages and the magic. The messages give you your hopes and aspirations but also prepares you for what's to come. When you glean into the soul, you can also enter the high stakes court of magic. Magic will happen with or without ever getting in tune with it. But at that point, all you can do is sit on the sidelines and WAIT, like everyone else until you can actually SEE IT, do its thing! Or, you can have a leap of faith and prepare yourself as if you were holding a catcher's mitt. Either way...the magic will give stellar performance!

9 GUIDES (SHORT VERSION)

Attached, you will find the worksheets that can help
you hone your skills. First start with prayer. Then
start with meditation. Also use the two concepts of
intra and ultra- gleaning to guide you while you
soul cleanse. Write the steps down. Repeat them, if
needed (record them whenever you notice a pattern
or event). Pray on it, to try and get a break through.
Be honest and sincere in your approach so that you
can see and feel the results. Getting Gods attention
will not be hard when it's done with honesty and

sincerity. These are matters of the heart and no one can deter you from faith's path but yourself. Seek God's attention in EVERYTHING that you do. And maybe you will get a break through (if you haven't already), like I did, as a gift. The gift of foresight I can claim, because it was given to me on the night of the sparkles when I stood (or kneeled) before God and God sent me an answer, that forever, in EVERYTHING-there will be MAGIC.

Peace and Love

Ihsan

Worksheet

Events, experiences, patterns:

Step # 1 write them down

1. First thing I noticed is_____

2. First time I wrote it down _____

3. How long has it been happening? _____

Methods that can help:

Step #2 methods that help

Intra-gleaning

How can I foster more awareness through intra-

gleaning? _____

Some of the things I've done are

_____

This made me feel…

_____

ADDENDUM

FOR THE LONG VERSION OF THE
WORKSHEETS (GRAPHS & TEXT),
PLEASE GO TO
WWW.IHSANJONES.COM

ABOUT THE AUTHOR

Ihsan Jones is a freelance writer that uses her experiences to explain unseen phenomena. Her dogma and style, dictated by her writing is amusing and fun as well as informative. She aims not only to please but to educate her audience in the only way she knows how-by telling the truth. Ihsan is a truth teller in her own right as witnessed through her experiences.